BROKEN
BUT NOT
FORGOTTEN

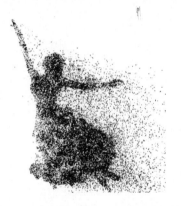

CLAUDIA BROWN-MCKENZIE

Broken: But Not Forgotten

Authored by Claudia Brown McKenzie

©Claudia Brown McKenzie 2023

Edited by Marcia M Publishing House Editorial Team

Published by Marcia M Spence of Marcia M Publishing House Ltd. West Bromwich, West Midlands, the UNITED KINGDOM B71 on behalf of Claudia Brown McKenzie.

Biblical references are taken from The King James Version, The Amplified Version and The New King James Version.

ISBN- 9781913905354 First Edition

A catalogue record for this book is available from the British Library

www.marciampublishing.com

ACKNOWLEDGEMENTS

I n every circumstance give thanks (1 Thessalonians 5:8 NKJ), it is with a grateful heart, I pen this acknowledgement to those who had been my tower of strength, my confidants, my encouragers and most of all, my prayer partners. No journey in life is ever one without a challenge and true to those words, this adventure has its own testimony of triumph, praise be to God. The Lord has been faithful to his word. He will perfect that which he has started. This book has been released. I give thanks to the Holy Spirit, who has directed me every step of the way, speaking so clearly in my spirit there was no room for doubt. He has sent destiny helpers and provided the resource to enable this vision. Lord Jesus, I give you praise.

I would like to acknowledge my husband, Trevor McKenzie, who has agreed for me to share, as I feel pleased. This book is not about blame, it is a true story of God's grace in our lives and a tool that is most used for future growth and development for others. Thank you to my sons, Hakim McKenzie and Jordan McKenzie who have been on the journey every step of the way, encouraging and assisting with the media and marketing strategy of the book. Thank you.

Thanks to my mom Angelena Brown, whose valuable contribution as a reader, encourager and confidant has been amazing. Thanks for sharing from your own experience of brokenness your encouraging words, "God **has a plan for every one of us"** those words cement deep in my heart, "**_The Lord will not give you more than you can bear._**"

Thank you.

Thanks to Sasha Gay-Smiths, author "Who is knocking" and Ann-Mare Royal, author "Reborn" who shared their own experience and knowledge base of writing and publishing their own books. I am extremely grateful.

Thanks to my brother Christopher Innerarity, my language coach and mentor, your contribution was extremely valuable to the success of this publication. Thank you.

Thanks to my church family, who have not ceased to pray and encourage me in order to make this dream a success.

Thanks to my siblings Andrae' Brown and Kevin Brown for your support, respectively.

Thank you, my readers, for joining me on this journey, your love and support is extraordinary, and my heart is truly grateful. Thank you for reading and I pray that your heart will be blessed by the contents of this book. Please share a copy with a friend.

God bless you.

ABOUT THE AUTHOR

 Claudia Brown-McKenzie is an entrepreneur, with two successful businesses. An active member in her church community, a wife of twenty-five years, a mother of two boys and most recently a grandmother. She worked previously as an early years educator, administrator, director and volunteers her service to many charities. Claudia enjoys the good times, travelling and spending time with family and friends, but her joy and aspiration is to touch and enrich the lives of young people. Most of her voluntary service is spent working in youth clubs, young offender institutes and Sunday school.

Mentoring and coaching young people in employability skills are her greatest dream and devotion; hence why she has established a youth employment scheme within her business. In this scheme, she enrolled young people from the age of sixteen to join her growing team, where young people are mentored and coached into their dream career paths. The drive was inspired from her own personal experience as a mother, a girl guide tutor, Sunday school teacher, mentor and coach. Claudia believes that young people have a hidden gem, and they just need someone with the right skills, patience and love to assist in their growth and development.

Claudia is a qualified Human Resource manager and develops skills within the workplace which enhances the team productivity.

The author strongly asserts that young people are often ignored based on their prior experience also their lack of knowledge. She has now noticed that gap and works tirelessly to fill it within the ethnic community businesses.

Prior to the new release of this book, writing was a distant dream. Claudia felt the urge to document her lived experience, but never in the terms of a diary or a book. Claudia says, *"I will not forget the process behind this journey, because it was through my testimony of refusing to compromise, lose my faith or change to the mindset of those around me, I stand victoriously. It would be very remiss of me to keep this story hidden because my faith and trust in God is the main reason, I choose to share some personal life-changing experiences I feel will benefit my readers.*

The emotional strain of feeling broken for years has been my disposition until I felt the courage in knowing though I am broken, I am certainly not forgotten."

CONTENTS

INTRODUCTION

Broken, *But Not Forgotten*, is the documentation of a divine encounter of God's presence. I sat down one morning in my living room, questioning the Lord about the various obstacles I faced as a Christian and, most of all, as a woman. Challenges that I had experienced through rejection and broken vows over the years. The level of rejection seemed unreal in most instances, and I asked the Lord 'why me?' I was not expecting a fairy tale story with a happy ever after ending, but nothing about my life seemed fair. I was broken unbelievably; it changed my personality and the ability to be

1

rational. I lost my light, the star that shined, the smile that lit the room. I was broken. So, as I put pen to paper, I wrote this book recounting brokenness and its emotional encounter that helps shape and structure one's ability, progression, and success.

Brokenness is classified as a psychological imbalance that affects a person's emotional state of mind. It reflects mainly on a significant life-changing experience that allows one to feel less than worthy and changes a person's outlook on life, and that is where my story began.

'They hated me without cause. I felt unloved, betrayed, and abandoned. Who is to be blamed? I ask myself countless times, I believe the lie, it was my fault, I wasn't pretty enough, nobody likes me, and the negative thoughts keep coming day after day until the answer comes through the affirmation by the Holy Spirit, my broken situation in life results from sin. I am not

bound to its core of self-defeating thoughts because God sent his Son, who was without sin, to be broken so that I might be healed.'

No matter how deep these feelings might be, no one can live a progressive life without broken experiences. It is the steppingstone to life-changing success.

Brokenness is actually a gift from God that shows his awesome and unyielding love. I could identify the infantile truth of Jesus Christ, how he practically reveals the true meaning of a broken life that brings forth growth, even through his death. He foretold the last importance of this body being broken for us, reflecting the transformation of his grace to us by his own broken experience.

Without brokenness, there is no room for restoration, a place to be made new, or a platform for growth. Christ's death has made it possible for us to transcend from brokenness to reconciliation and be healed.

Broken But Not Forgotten is a calculative review of my personal testimony whilst exploring the theoretical background of brokenness.

Brokenness is essential for growth, but we often find people who struggle to even move beyond the lifestyle they now come to adapt to as the norm. I asked questions such as '*what is my God-given assignment, and how can I fulfil it?*' My assignment hid in the secret place of the Most High; it's through our intimate moments that God reveals his plan to those who abide in his presence.

I pray you will find the courage and strength to emerge from your brokenness into his divine assignment for your life. This book inspires and encourages others whilst we are broken; God has not forgotten us.

MY BROKENNESS

I can do all things through Christ who strengthens me (Philippians 4:13). This quote from the scripture categorically evaluates my profile as a woman, wife, and mother. I was born on the sunny island of Jamaica, the second child of my parents, Ronald and Angelena Brown, who raised five children in the fear of the Lord and contended for the faith to maintain a godly home. By their example of faith and steadfastness in the word of God and by training their children in the fear of the Lord Jesus Christ, at the tender age of fifteen, I answered the call.

The event leading up to my baptism was a direct intervention of God's immense grace and power. I had no intention of surrendering my life to Christ at the time; I was just a teenager with a curious mind, but God had a plan.

It was Good Friday, and I attended church as I usually do during Easter. During the ceremony, I felt convicted by the word as I made the bold step into the unknown of God's will. I could hear the chatter of my friends but something amazing was taking place and I could not help myself and so I surrendered.

God's ultimate plan and desire was that this was the appointed moment that hell would belch and release my soul from captivity. I hesitated, not. I responded as though my life depended on that very moment. It was like, if I had let that moment pass, there wouldn't be another opportunity given again. In total surrender, I bowed my knees and prayed unto the Lord of all ages. My life was transformed, and I experienced a new level of life in the abundance of God's grace.

It has been over twenty years since that day, and I have no regrets. On the contrary, I strive daily to live as an example so that my children, my husband, my siblings and my acquaintances may emulate.

Upon my conversion, I wasted no time developing my spiritual and social skills in leadership by enrolling on the church activities programme. As a new believer in Christ, I quickly recognised my calling as an intercessor. I joined the fasting and prayer team alongside the local youth choir, the new believers' bible study programme and the children's ministry.

My local church was my refuge. It was where everybody was somebody, and the youth department flourished beyond our expectations. I first recognised the gift of dancing in the presence of God back in Jamaica. I used the initiative to organise a dance group for the Girl Guide Association. The street evangelising team, Family Training department and daily Vacation Bible School were some departments I worked in. I was living my best life, but there was still a need for companionship, so I did what I knew best: I prayed. I asked the Lord to send me a husband. A godly man, an intercessor, an encourager, a destiny helper, a listener, a friend, one that loves the Lord and most of all, a people person. I prayed in December 1994, and by January 1995, I met my husband in the most unusual setting I would have never imagined. Ideally, I was hoping we would have met at church, convention, rally etc., but I was on the job. I was the newest member of the team of cashiers at my local supermarket, and you know, as the newbie, you always get the odd job. So, I had to cover for another staff member on this particular day. When he walked in and interrupted my meditation with the Lord on the job. It was a quiet morning, and I was busy taking a few minutes to say how much I love the Lord and just reflecting on his goodness whilst glancing over at a Christian magazine, *The Challenge,* I was annoyed at first, but my annoyance quickly submerged once I realised that he too knew about the magazine I suddenly became convinced that he too was acquainted with the faith movement and we engaged in conversation.

Our friendship grew, and we began visiting each other's churches. We had so much in common. The first date we ever had was at a prayer meeting because we were both intercessors. We spent hours talking about our future of getting married, our ministry and the importance of prayer, why we pray and the result of our prayer. What was significant about our relationship and our common interest was that we both sang on the choir at our respective churches, and we enjoyed swinging our legs, so it was no issue when we had a youth competition at my church, and we required male dancers to complete our group. He was excited and full of life and zeal for the things of the Lord. I was smitten by his love, his charm, and his devotion to the Lord. I was Ruth, and he was my Boaz and so our hearts melted for each other and in 1997 we sealed our relationship in the company of our family and friends. Everything was simply perfect.

What could go wrong? We were young and full of life. Our relationship was solid. We both loved the Lord and were equally committed to our respective areas in the ministry, ever ready to serve. We enjoyed each other's company and desired to share that love with another, so in January 1999, we had our first son. He was the apple of our eyes, the centre of our earthly joy, and we loved and adored him with the little we could afford.

We were new to this new world of parenting, but we wanted to give our son the absolute best of what we could afford. Being a new mother, I no longer had the privilege of working as before. We could not afford childcare, so we searched further afield for a new job opportunity. The opportunity arises through an invitation from his mom and in July 2000, to travel to the UK. Our journey together took an unexpected turn, but our faith remains intact and so we prayed about it and moved into our new direction of growth.

In December 2000, I emigrated to the United Kingdom to join my husband, and life changed from the norm. My oldest son, Hakim, was almost two years old when I arrived in this strange country. I had no family or friends apart from my husband and my in-laws. I was apprehensive, but my faith kept me going and the Lord promised he would never leave me, so I was encouraged. However, on my arrival, things seemed odd. My husband seemed different to

11

me. He had grown his hair and had two gold teeth plus an additional ring alongside our wedding band. As I was on edge, I started to pray and ask the Lord for directions. The comforting word of the Lord was my rock and shield. I had to rely totally on God because he knew the beginning from the end. He is a faithful God with promise.

This wasn't our plan; the script changed without notice, so I needed clarity. I just didn't recognise him. Once we had time to speak, I was curious to find out what was going on. Maybe he was experiencing a midlife crisis, and everyone forgot to tell me about it. I was not expecting any of the above. I asked about church, but he could not point me in the direction of a church. His choice of music changed; prayer was never again our favourite topic. It was as if we had nothing in common.

I was confused about how a man could change so drastically in less than six months. I had more questions than answers. My husband spent time together with some guys from our island, lost his focus, and wasn't rationalising his priority. So, our common stamping ground was left on the back burner. The very source that tied us together originally was no longer a key factor. He no longer wanted to pray. Our fellowship dried up. He was distracted, and my voice became that of the nagging wife. I was so confused that I went into a sudden depression that held me captive for many years. Without knowing why, I was so low in my spirit and why my tears were my only comfort.

For years I failed to connect with my husband; I felt neglected, abandoned, and rejected. Nothing about me was attractive to him anymore. I was a scared woman lost in my pain without hope while caring for a son who struggled to speak at almost four years old. To add to my dilemma, I was expecting another son. I cried more than I could pray. I tried to function normally at church because I was afraid to let others see my pain.

My marriage suffered a horrible death because I could no longer reach the man I loved. He had somehow stopped loving me, his heart was stolen, and there was absolutely nothing I could do about it. Lies became our truth, infidelity strongly moved into our union,

I was broken, I could not differentiate between what was true or what was a lie. I was constantly being told that I was making an accusation with no evidence to support my arguments. I felt stupid and confused. By this time, I could not assert myself any longer.

I had lost my confidence and struggled to make friends, so I resigned to this as the norm. I held my head in silence, thinking, *God must have forgotten me*.

For a while, I was in denial about what was going on. Then, as I sat down one day, the tears ran down my cheeks; without knowing where to go or what to do next, I questioned the Lord, *why me? What have I done to deserve this kind of cruel act?* I complained before God, and I remember my son saying in pure innocence and love, 'Mom, you are on the motorway and about to exit, don't lose focus.' Oh, my God. Those words pierced my heart as I melted before him in shame, and I repented. Then I remembered Job. *Should I only expect good and not evil from the Lord? Don't my trials bear fruit to my testimony? Why should I continue to be ashamed?*

I am only human, Oh God, and even as I try to be strong, but Lord, my weakness has held me captive. Nothing makes sense. I am hurting deep within, but I will trust you, Lord, even when the storm is raging. Amen.

Finally, I took baby steps on the road to recovery, and God sent a friend with whom I could share my story. She was blown away with awe. With her connection, I could regulate my status with my husband, Yes, the same man who had been so mean, but God's love makes the difference.

Could it be that the lord would have kept me to be an instrument of glory in this present situation? I have tried so many times to escape the prison of my marriage, but I wasn't released to go. The very person who caused me some of my greatest pain, the Lord, placed to help me weather the storms in my darkest hour.

I didn't have the heart to harm him though I knew how, but God was strengthening me even though I didn't realise it. Most astonishing was that this battle wasn't physical but spiritual, and though many times I hit the floor, I felt the hand of God holding me close.

Even in my brokenness, the Lord kept telling me that his grace was enough for me, that I should stay on board, and no life would be lost. I was becoming more frustrated under the pressure. Instead of things getting better, they were getting worse, and I could not understand why the Lord kept saying, *'stay the course.'* Then the Lord drew me to the story of Hosea's unfaithful wife, as the stronghold on her life kept her going back to the place of whoredom, disgrace and shame. Then I began researching the background of my husband's family tree and realised that this behaviour was inherited, and he had allowed himself to be a candidate to take on his father's shame. His behaviour became worse once his dad passed away. It was only then that I realised that this was the enemy's plan, so he devised a devious plan. The enemy does not want to see the will of the Lord in our life; therefore, he makes every attempt to kill it before it sprouts. I remember one night after leaving university and heading home, with all the suppressing thoughts swirling around my head, I was driving on the opposite side of the dual carriageway heading to Birmingham. Had it not been for another motorist alerting me of the danger that night, I would not be here telling my story. In everything, God is faithful. I was pushed to my limit, but I trusted that somehow, I would smile again, not knowing how, but my faith kept me.

Leaving my homeland with little education and moving to a strange land, I was determined to succeed. I got my Batchelors degree in Business and Human Resource Management , in 2014 and a year later, a master's degree. The journey to complete my first degree was so horrifying I lost my dissertation one and a half weeks before submission. There was no trace of it on my hard drive, email, university E-portal or laptop. It was as if it had never been there, but I kept hearing the Holy Spirit gently speaking, saying write it again. I almost lost my mind, but he kept repeating the same command. Start writing again. Amid the confusion, I heard myself arguing back at the voice. *I can't do this in just one week; it's too much! I won't be able to redo the work! I have spent the last six months working on in such a short time.* The voice repeated the same direction, 'start writing again.' I had no other option, I simply obeyed and to God be the glory; I finished on time for submission. Over the past few months, I have struggled to find data. I did so well on that piece of work that the university offered me a scholarship to write my master's. The enemy thought he had me bound and destroyed, but God had a plan. The scripture is true to the end. All things work for the good of those who love the Lord.

The journey has been one of a roller-coaster, and the vision to be the best of who I am has been an uphill struggle. After junior school, I have always desired to achieve academically; despite my best effort, my attempts seemed fruitless. The vision was still my goal, and no matter the challenge, I was determined to fulfil a long-awaited vision. In 2014, I achieved my degree and a year later my masters.

In 2022, we celebrated our 25th wedding anniversary; we testify that the Lord has restored us in double for our shame. Our little family has grown as we welcome our first grandson, charming and beautiful. Even with this wonderful blessing, the enemy ceases not his plan to create confusion, but our prayer remains daily before the Lord, and he hears our cry and answer by fire. Hallelujah!

Today, I run and operate one of the most popular Caribbean Takeaways within my region. I could also rebrand my boutique and expand my distribution to bridal-wear and accessories along with my husband, mentor my children to set up their own businesses and encourage them to trust God. This accomplishment I do not take for granted. God's favour (Yahweh) has shined down on me. I was broken by my circumstances, yet he loves me. I was crushed under all the heat, but he did not forget me. He restored me and made me whole. I am grateful; by this, I live my life not feeling ashamed of my past but rejoicing in God's abundant mercies.

Prayer

Heavenly Father, I thank you for this experience. I would like to thank you for allowing me to be sent forth as a minister of your grace. Thank you, that through my brokenness, generational curses have been broken. The lessons learned through this experience have given insight into your amazing grace, thank you, Lord. Thank you for your boldness to speak and not be afraid. Thank you for the heart that will be encouraged through this message. In Jesus' Holy name, I pray. Amen.

MORE THAN BROKEN

To be able to say that you are more than broken, one first has to acknowledge the reality of the unfadeable truth of brokenness; the place where dreams, relationships and trusts have been lost.

In the circle of life, we hear about some remarkable stories of ordinary people who have overcome the odds through broken dreams and aspirations. Their experiences have helped them to climb every mountain and scale over every valley to get to the plain. The challenges they face mould their characteristics and fuel their growth and development.

There is no life-changing experience without challenge, no success without a story and no victory without a battle, but the scenario changes once it is injected with faith. Having confidence and hope in the unseen gives a simple analysis of how our faith in a time of brokenness and hopelessness guides us through challenging situations. Faith enables us to see through the dark clouds and envision a path to a brighter and more fruitful tomorrow. A future where we can see the fruition of our faith in action based on the challenges we face; guarantees us the testimony of victory yet not seen (Hebrews 11:1).

My brokenness blurred my vision for a while, and I lost all sense of direction, but my faith in God allowed me to testify of his goodness, and his grace gave me hope. Hope that gave me the strength to say yes. This hurdle has broken my confidence, but there is light through the cracks, and I will survive.

I can now reflect and analyse the emotional struggle and pain I faced during that time.

I am not afraid to testify that I had a tough time in my marriage. I never thought I could have made it. My hope was dashed to pieces, but God's grace kept me. I now feel the strength to share from a place of confidence in God that he can do far more than I can imagine or think.

There are celebrities and prominent members of society who share their stories of triumph that touch the hearts of every listener, giving great comfort and encouragement. Sir Nelson Mandela is one of those persons I have grown to admire and respect for his braveness and renowned character, and his faith in God as a believer. His life touched many across the world. An inspiring young activist who God has used as an instrument to encourage and strengthen others who served in public offices in our society. Brokenness has no bondage; we see how this man was robbed of his dignity and imprisoned for many years by those who inflict the hardest blow but the God in him has given him the strength to forgive. This strength didn't come out by the desire of man's ability but from the gift of God that speaks hope that though we might be broken by our experience, this is not the end of our book, it's only another chapter. We are so much more than just broken people; we will be made whole.

Looking back at our struggle we might have been deprived of some basic need, but God's promises is sure in our times of great affliction and brokenness. This reality might not seem like the norm for others because we live in a world where people wear masks to conceal the pain of last night's nightmare. With our stubborn will and revengeful attitude, we refuse to forgive.

Others struggle deeply with the thought of looking back on the pain that has engulfed their lives and enslaved them for years. The thought of forgiving those who might have wronged us is an uphill struggle for many, and food for thought. It is a journey worth advancing if we are to be healed.

Growing up, I often heard the old folks saying, 'in going forward, one must remember where they are coming from,' and it's amazing how these simple but effective words inspire my analytical thinking. Those little gems we often take for granted truly yield the message of truth, food for thought.

We sometimes have to focus on the lesson that in the future means we must take a step backwards and reflect before advancing. The reflection process allows us to regather our thoughts and assess the situation before continuing.

This is an extraordinary example of maturity, an amazing attribute that can only be revealed through the strength of the Lord. Only when we have mastered these obstacles, we can honestly say, "I am more than just broken."

Despite the horrifying process, brokenness is part of our growth and development, and no one wants to be broken. The scripture speaks of brokenness in the future tense as the transition that helps us to be better. In our brokenness we have a great desire to turn to God to navigate through our storms. This is a sacrifice worth its weight in gold (Psalm 51:17 NIV), My sacrifice, Oh God, is a broken spirit; a broken and contrite heart you, God, will not despise. David is qualified to write this Psalm because he too, has suffered a great deal of brokenness and rejection. Still, he learns that if he humbles himself before God and seeks forgiveness for his error, he will also learn and be made whole.

We live in a world where our stubborn will and revengeful attitude causes us to refuse to forgive. Still, if we cannot face that painful situation through the lens of God's eternal love, then we will continue to live as slaves to the thing that broke us.

Brokenness is a lonely road, but it is where we learn the most vital lesson of forgiveness and the strength to move on. As we navigate through the storms of life, we often wonder where God is and how he could allow such a thing to happen. Yet a most common phrase is often asked, 'why me, God?' on second thought, *why not me God?* This was the reaction of Job to the question asked by his wife. Job's wife questioned his faith in God, and her word was not encouraging (Job 2:10).

In everything, there has to be a balance, we cannot have one without the other, yet we cry and complain when the storms of loneliness, sadness and brokenness appear. The writer of

Purpose of This Storm, Nadia Nembhard-Hunt, mentions that some of the storms we face are designed by God. They are there for our personal development and growth. When I look back and see how far I have come, I cease not to be grateful to God who kept me. Jeremiah 29:11 states that God's thoughts for us are for good and not evil. The storms we are presently facing are not there to destroy us but to bring about an expected future. He has our best interest at heart, and we need not be afraid. In the story in Mark 6:45-53, we see Jesus telling his disciples to go into a boat, into a storm, while he sends the crowd away. The scripture says that around the fourth watch, Jesus came walking on water and he spoke to them, 'be not afraid it is I, be not afraid.' One writer wrote a colourful analysis of this story that really grabbed my attention. He said, 'Jesus knew that his ragamuffin followers were not ready to receive his promise.' Hence, he had to send them out into the deep to convince them of his mighty power at work.

Sometimes too much sunshine breathes laziness and complacency, and we lack the faith and trust needed to mobilise our growth. The Apostle Paul often speaks of his thorn in the flesh as a constant reminder of God's goodness and faithfulness as he goes through his storms (2 Corinthians 12:7). Reading those words was an astonishing revelation, our storms will not abort God's plan for our lives, his promise for our lives will abide forever. At the peak of my storms, I could not deny that a level of brokenness, had invaded my life, that I couldn't comprehend. I was miserable, confused, heartbroken and alone.

As I lay my head on my pillow, I complained and arose each morning asking myself, *'why me, God?'* Here comes that quest of self-pity, fear and doubt. This continued for years until I realised, I didn't want to remain in this situation; feeling sorry for myself, There must be more, I needed to live, I needed to be seen to be remembered. My heart and soul cried out for more! So, I got up from my place of Lo-debar. I accepted the invitation to be refreshed at the king's table. Getting up is not easy, not when you have grown to accept your situation as it is. It takes courage, a transformed mindset, and the power of God to get up and be raised in confidence. We see in the story of the prodigal son he first had to have a conversation with himself, recognising that he was in a bad state, but there was hope beyond his brokenness. So, he arose.

Being more than just broken should be our daily pledge. Everyone has a story of a broken situation. No matter who they are or their status, we all have issues. It is often easier to oblige through brokenness and remain confined to our brokenness rather than getting up. Some of us struggle to move past that pain, that storm, that heartbreak, that rejection and that betrayal. All this negative energy is part of the process that summarises broken experiences, but there is hope. Our brokenness shapes our character and strengthens our faith. So, don't say it shouldn't have happened to me. On the contrary, it was essential for your growth and maturity, which seems implausible to many of us.

Accept your brokenness as the testing of our faith. God tested Abraham in Genesis 22; such testing ought to cause us to seek a deeper and spiritual upliftment at a time when we are vulnerable and fragile, and we need a tower of strength that is mightier and stronger than our human effort. I hereby attest that spiritual upliftment is key when the storms of life rage against us. We need an anchor that can provide the support mechanism that will enable us to weather the storm.

Prayer

Heavenly Father, thank you for being there every step of the way. We glorify your name, Lord. You are our strength (2 Corinthians 12:9), when we face difficulties and hopeless experiences. You are the lifter of our head and a present help in time of trouble (Psalm 46:1). Lord, thank you for being there when no one else could. Lord, thank you for the lessons learned through our broken situations and the strength you have given us to move beyond them. Heavenly Father, we honour you today that despite the shame, we can use our experience to encourage and testify of your great power at work in our lives. Help us reaffirm your promise every day and remind us that our past holds no condemnation to those who belong to Christ Jesus (Romans 8:1), because we are set free in you. Therefore, we celebrate our God is faithful in everything. Amen.

Defining brokenness

Before we can define brokenness, we first need to establish the correct definition of brokenness through the spectrum of a wider audience. The Bible defines brokenness as total surrender to the Spirit of God to be used by him. Brokenness in the natural realm means breaking apart the norms or a pattern that affects the human mind's physical, psychological, and emotional physics.

Many writers and researchers describe brokenness in our lives as an aspect of hopeless encounters; people feel so rejected that accepting the loss is the safest option. This mindset eliminates any hope of restoration, and the individual is left alone with many undesirable thoughts that will eliminate their conception of hope or restoration. I was amazed by a post sent to me which read, 'broken crayons still colour,' the very statement spoke value to my situation. In that moment, I reflected on all my broken dreams, promises, and self-worth. When I studied the quote, I couldn't hold back the tears or the emotion that paralysed my state of mind, and I felt lifeless, hopeless, ashamed, and totally broken. I ponder the thought; *how can I really emerge from this grave of emotional helplessness? 'Is there really any hope for me?'* was the voice screaming within. I felt that my life had been an uphill struggle from the beginning. No matter how much I tried to escape, I never could shift the reality that, somehow, I am tied to this brokenness issue. I now soon realised that it was a spiritual stronghold that kept me captive.

As a young graduate who had just left school and started college in Jamaica, my personality perplexed me; I had no self-confidence; I was simply confused. As I struggled to contextualise the English language, my tutor once said, 'I am praying for you.' For years, those words haunted me. I just couldn't understand what she saw in me or what she had envisioned, but I couldn't bring it out. The struggle continued for many years before I could dismantle the puzzle and start all over again.

In the analyses presented, there seems to be an emotional bond or a spiritual alliance that refuses to let go of the stronghold it has. I have now realised that the enemy is very strategic in his scheme, and his intention is to kill, steal and destroy (John 10:10-29); he depicts an active source or a platform to rejoice, and he will stop at nothing to execute his plan.

I have learned that the basic principle in surviving brokenness is to trust the true and living God, who knows all about our weaknesses. Trusting God means relying on him to help us put the pieces back together, heal our brokenness, and mend our broken hearts and minds. For the first time in my life, it was clear my brokenness did not mean all was lost. On the contrary, I was stretched to maximise my full potential. I just did not know it then.

All the emotional baggage, self-doubt, insecurity and the psychological fear and instability sweats on the outside, I felt as if I had maximised all my strength, when as though all hope was lost a gush of energy emerged from deep within my soul. A move that revived my confidence in God and reminds me that no matter what I face, he is Lord over every challenge and situation. I reflect on the struggles I met with my eldest son, he could not talk, and up to the age of four, it seemed as if all hope were lost. I was in the position of the woman with the issue of blood in Matthew 9:20-22. I visited all the speech therapists in my locality. Nothing happened after we followed the prescribed exercises and therapy sessions. My precious child could not speak at all. My heart was crushed because the child who was walking and teething as early as six months was not speaking as other children in his year. That experience left me baffled, and I had to encourage myself in the word of the Lord.

Feeling isolated, in a bubble of brokenness, loneliness, and pain, there was nobody I knew who could relate to my pain. I clearly recall sitting in my bedroom, getting dressed, and my son tried to explain something he had done the day before at school, but he had no words. I was frustrated, but also was so righteously vindicated in the spirit. I called my son to come to me; It was then I declared in the name of our Lord Jesus Christ for him to speak it out! That was day one of the miracles. On day two, I repeated my actions, singing and having devotion on the go, when my son (the very son who could not speak a day before) called out to me in plain English as I sang and made a joyful noise unto the Lord. 'Mom!' he shouted. 'Stop the noise. You are annoying me!' I was utterly astonished by what I heard! My son spoke for the very first time in the four years of his life.

In that moment when I felt completely hopeless, the Holy Spirit moved upon my heart with power and clarity, and I spoke the words that brought the fruit my heart had so long awaited. My pain, shame and frustration about my son's speech was redeemed. The Holy Spirit moved in such a way in my life that I never expected, and the victory was won. This experience was my first true miracle encounter, it testifies that God is able to do just what he said he will do. The promises are definite, and he is a God that cannot lie.

As I reflected, I recalled the story of Ezekiel, the prophet. He was a young priest and served the Lord faithfully for many years before God told him he would be the prophet of his people. Not long after his assignment, he received warnings from the Lord regarding his people, signs which were not well received. To add to his dilemma, he was a refugee and a slave in Babylon. Ezekiel encountered rejection by his people. He felt alone as all the other prophets were dead. The city lay in ruins, the temple destroyed, and all hope seemed lost. At his lowest point, he also experienced God's power in the valley of dry bones (Ezekiel 37). He was confused when God brought him to the valley of dry bones, a place of hopelessness, a place of lifelessness, to reveal his ultimate power of grace and favour to him. Everything was dead, the bones were bleach-bone dry, and nothing breathed, and God asked him, 'can these dry bones live?' And he responded, 'O Sovereign Lord, You alone know the answer to that.' And as the Lord commanded Ezekiel to speak to those lifeless bones, something astonishing unfolded. The bones of each body came together and attached themselves as they had been before. The muscle and flesh began to form over the bones and skins covering the body, and God allowed the breath of life to reclaim those who were dead and lived again (Ezekiel 37:1-10). So, God opens the graves of the dead and allows them to rise again in the newness of life. His love is unchangeable, and it is his promise to his people he is forever faithful.

Amid all the chaos, God brought hope through my lived experience, a hope that makes me not ashamed (Romans 5:4–5). God breathed life into a dead nation, and their hope was restored.

What a powerful encounter to have when you least expect a positive result from a broken and lifeless experience; restoration is birthed. The prophet's confidence was restored and demonstrated in his response. Our relationship with God expresses such testimony and confidence as we seek his strength each day for guidance and direction.

Brokenness had held me captive in a paralysed condition for years. I simply could not shake off the chains that held me bound for so long; it was as if I had stopped living, and tears dispersed. Bitterness, pain, loneliness, and frustration had engulfed my life. I simply could not move beyond this crisis.

I had not given up on my faith, but I lacked the basic understanding of activating the very promise I preach. My relationship with God was not being strengthened daily in prayer and devotion. I stopped praying and I chose the easy option, to live in fear. I felt lost, lonely and afraid, without hope or direction. How could this ever be true? My faith was the only thing I had left, and even the thought of progressing beyond my personal conflict was a distant dream. I was bonded to broken dreams, low self-esteem and fear; my life was in total shambles.

Suddenly, when I least thought about it, a glimmer of light flashed across my path; the clay that blinded my vision had been removed, and I was able for the first time to see. The story in John nine of the man who was blind for many years resigned deeply to my spirit; as the clay fell off my eyes, it became clear how wasted my life had become. It was like I fell asleep, and all this weight had become my disposition. I had come to my senses, like the prodigal son in Luke 15:17, after years of eating with the pigs. The power of God found me and brought restoration that could be found nowhere else but by his grace. In that moment, I refused to be broken; I embraced the promises of freedom that came only through Christ, my saviour. I changed my disposition and repositioned my energy and thoughts on things that are positive, lovely, trustworthy, and of good report. The scripture Philippians 4:8 encourages us to think about these things. I now understand that regaining a positive mindset requires a continuous focus on the things of God, forgetting those things or situations that have contributed to my past. I decided to 'press towards the mark for the prize of the high calling of God in Christ Jesus' (Philippians 3:14) and stay focused on his promises.

The battle to regain progressiveness beyond brokenness begins in the mind. The mind is the place of intellectual reasoning; it is a spiritual platform, and if not guarded by the power of God, the enemy can easily control it. In her first series of *Commanding Your Morning*, Dr Cindy Trimm refers to the active mind as a transformation of the spoken word we verbalised. She continues to illustrate that our behaviour is based on the information that first occurs in our minds. Human behaviour is revealed by the thought process of the mind. It is no wonder the adversary wastes no time seeking a pathway of trying to control and manipulate our actions through his scheme of deception. The scripture speaks intensively about the renewed mind in Romans 12:2, because it is the gateway to the soul. The scripture expounds on the importance of a sound mind and why we must keep it intact with God's divine plans. If the mind is not protected by a spiritual source that will enable it to develop and progress, it is left vulnerable to any attack from the enemy.

Prayer

Lord, we stop to reflect on the many trials you brought us over, hallelujah! We could have lost our mind, but you kept us amid every trial and so we thank you. Lord, we glory in your presence because you are indeed in control of our minds. Your word declares that we should be transformed by the renewing of our mind (Romans 12:2). Heavenly Father, we recognise that transformation can only occur through your word. Therefore, we now decree and declare your word of hope right now in our broken situation. We activate your promise in our life right now in the name of Jesus Christ. Amen.

CHARACTERISTICS OF BROKENNESS

B rokenness changes a person's behaviour pattern whether he or she practises a faith-centred relationship or not. The ultimate goal in dealing with brokenness is solely dependent on the source of our strength and how we balance life's issues. Another key point to highlight are the lessons learned. No experience should be wasted, no matter how painful, because it is essential for our growth and development. Therefore, though we might try to hide our brokenness and remain in isolation, it is only beneficial once the silence is broken. Too often, people think they can weather the storms they face independently by seeking an alternative solution, such as sex, fame, drugs, money, and career path, rather than turning to God who knows all about us and who knows all our cares. Many have learned the harsh reality that brokenness leads to spiritual imbalance and can only be restored through the power of the Holy Spirit. When people face a crisis, they usually turn to faith when there is no other option. We see this sample principle displayed by the apostle Paul, a prominent member of Rome who served as a Pharisee, a scholar and a Roman soldier. His prestige and eloquent background had no value when he came face to face with his own broken situation. Paul's brokenness with the thorn in his flesh was ongoing. So, he sought God to deliver him from his struggle. Still, as he looked straight into the face of God for help, he was reassured with words of consolation. Words that many

47

today draw comfort from and continue to echo throughout our struggles, 'your grace is sufficient for me,' (2 Corinthians 12:9). I believe he was wounded, broken and ashamed. Too scared even to mention it, but God's grace kept him humble, though broken but not crushed, perplexed but not driven to despair, persecuted but not forsaken (2 Corinthians 4:8).

Brokenness, along with all its other emotional baggage, brings along with itself shame, guilt and fear that hold us ransom for years. I, too, can testify to that because I am a survivor. I struggled to escape because I was too ashamed to tell others about my situation and how it affected me. Shame that allowed me to see my situation as an isolated one that I was too afraid to share. I recognised that without my faith in God, I would still be bound to the crutches that stole my laughter. My testimony of overcoming the trials has given me the confidence to shout aloud, 'I am renewed, and I am set free to laugh. My mourning has turned into joy!'

It is difficult to imagine the transformation from a disposition of brokenness to wholeness without a faith-centred relationship; it's so easy to accept the harsh reality of your present pain as the norm. Your ultimate escape from your brokenness depends on your core strength and belief system.

When your faith is not tied to a positive source whereby you can see your brokenness as a stretching tool for growth and development. In that case, you will definitely feel the shame and reproach of your pain. However, we need not be ashamed of our past; it is a process that helps mould our character and strengthen our faith, to believe that though, it was tough, I made it because of whom I believe in. The Elohim, God who preserves (Genesis 17:7), Yahweh-Nissi, 'the Lord my banner' and The Lord is my rock, my fortress, my deliverer. (Psalm 18:2.) He is our source of strength in the midst of our storms, his word is the seed that is planted in our spirit, which enables us to trust him when all hope is lost.

Our faith, intellect, and understanding are tied to our spirit. We are not just physical but also spiritual beings made in God's image (Genesis 2). So, our faith will work as a catalyst that helps us know there is hope; God has not forgotten us, and his strength works best in our brokenness to give us that expected end. Without that assurance, it is easy to stray and live on the edge of destruction because there is no safety net for where to turn or who to lean on during dark times. But if you believe God is in control of everything though you fall, your faith remains intact and firm.

When your faith is firmly rooted in God, you will portray a godly character and behave differently through times of brokenness from those who show no faith. We often seek solutions in other means when there is a crisis because brokenness profoundly changes you as a person, but it is our faith that aids us through the process.

In attempting to even evaluate the different behaviour patterns of a broken individual, we first need to establish the root of the unbelief or lack of faith. Brokenness or failure has forced many people to lose hope in everything, including God. It is as if they sever their spiritual connection to God because of a traumatic experience.

A friend once shared a quote that captured my thoughts: 'brokenness is a recurrent activity that affects the mind, which creates an imbalance in how we process circumstances as they arise. Studies show this is a key issue that affects our cognitive thinking and stimulates mental illness; as we explore this topic, be encouraged; you will not lose it because Jehovah Shalom is our peace.' When we encounter the peace of God, brokenness becomes a distant memory.

Individuals who do not practise a faith-centred relationship seek a physical solution to the pain or hurt they constantly face. Their dependency can become abusive to the holistic man as the soul's hunger is starving because of their lack of faith.

Research identifies that persons who experience deep levels of brokenness turn to alcohol, drugs, sex, gambling, or other substance abuse intending to escape. Unfortunately, none of these actions offer a safe escape but a suppressing motion in denying the true reality.

As I studied the tri-part nature of man, I understood that man is body, soul, and spirit. The soul is self-consciousness, which helps to develop our personality and form our identity through our emotions as we can resolve, choose, and decide. The spirit is God's consciousness, which is the inner organ that connects us with our creator (John 4:24). There is no other creature that is created with its inner connection with God, hence why having a constant dialogue and fellowship will help us strengthen our relationship with him daily. Then there is the body, which is sense-conscious, processing the physical element of man using the five senses and the world that revolves around him. This analysis identifies a greater need for man than for its physical needs. The physical cannot satisfy the need of the spirit because the needs differ and require a different source of satisfaction. In the scripture, the tri-part nature of man, 'the body,' is not mentioned as a key factor as the other two elements. Why is that? I ask. Could it be that the body's significance is less important than the spirit or the soul, which is connected to God? When we view the scriptures, we see where the body is rotten and decays as the remains of man are buried. It returns to the ground from which it was taken (Genesis 2:7); the body's life span is limited according to Psalm 90:10; because of sin, it cannot live beyond its set time. The physical body will not endure beyond this present period. However, the spirit of man lives because this mortal flesh shall put on immortality. We shall be changed (1 Corinthians 15:54). Yet we often overlook this concept and seek to satisfy the physical and neglect of our spirit man, which remains unnourished. Let us know that when God created man, he made him in his own image (Genesis 1:26-27) and breathed the breath of life into man. He became a living soul (Genesis 2:7). Therefore, every part of the holistic man needs to be ministered to and not neglected.

The soul comprises the mind, man's will, and emotion. The characteristic of man is embedded in his soul and spirit, which is the only way we can communicate with God. In our communication with God, our spirit relates to him through worship; according to John 4:24, *'God is spirit, and those who worship Him must worship in spirit and truth.'* Therefore, when we deny our soul the satisfaction of spiritual encounters, man is incomplete as a being. According to the study by God's own heart "the world is inherently a spiritual world. The things we see are not just composed of the physical; many are visible in the spirit that our natural eyes cannot see. *Trying to separate the three components will be devastating.*

If our faith is concentrated on God, our spiritual being is refreshed daily as we encounter his presence. But, on the other hand, when our physical tri-nature part of man takes pre-eminence in our lives, there will be avoidance, and man will always seek another source to fill it. It is shocking how this knock-on effect weighs us down with self-defeating thoughts, another active motion that emerges from the ground root of the mind. Hence, the spirit of God must protect our mind; otherwise, it is left vulnerable to any attack.

In my line of business, my staff are at constant risk for accidents at the drop-of-a-hat because we are in a kitchen filled with sharp objects. Therefore, all workplaces must have a First Aid Kit and an accident book; both kit and handbook are next to the work surface, not tucked away in some corner. Some use these items daily to record an accident, from a burn to a cut. Therefore, incidents must be treated and documented. If a cut or burn is left untreated, the consequences can harm the business and the individual. Thus, the same principle applies in a broken situation. To grow beyond our own personal brokenness, we must first deal with the root cause of the issue; sometimes, we must revisit the place where it all began so that we can deal with it accordingly. This process is not an immediate solution but a gradual move that can only be accomplished through his abundant grace. The struggle is real, but there is a place of refuge in the presence of the Lord where his strength is made perfect in our weakness (2 Corinthians 12:9). Be encouraged.

Prayer

Heavenly Father, thank you for being close to the broken-hearted and wounded soul (Psalms 51:17). You attend to their cry, Lord our faith, that helps us to not shy away but to come boldly before the throne room of grace whereby we cry Abba Father.

We thank you for the ability to be transparent about our brokenness and to identify the unique character traits that have been developed. Lord, we now understand that though it has been a painful experience, Lord, you have kept us. We can use our stories as a catalyst to help support and encourage others that your grace is sufficient to keep us (2 Corinthians 12:9). Lord, help us understand even in our wilderness experience, we have the confidence to say that "we know that all things God works for the good of those who love him, who have been called according to his purpose" (Romans 8:28 Int). We may not understand the process, but we know without any doubt that you are working it out for our good. So, we take this opportunity to be thankful for your grace, love, and faithfulness. We decree you are our strength and present help in times of trouble (Psalm 46:1). Today, Lord, we make our boast in you, hallelujah! Amen.

COPING WITH BROKENNESS

O ur brokenness will eliminate us from every level of control; it paralyses our ability to move beyond this point, hence why we have to be strategic if we are to move beyond broken situations and circumstances. I could not ignore the parable in Matthew 19:16-24 of the rich man wanting the ability to be in control of his destiny and personal affairs. This shift changes the direction of power. We can see how his position enables him to navigate all the players. Power allows persons to act superior to another because they can instigate certain authority.

And just like a rainbow, it was clear he had a blind spot; he could not see beyond his wealth. The tripartite nature of the spirit man was starving; because he allowed his physical side to remain dominant, he failed to see how important the lack of spiritual connection was to his holistic man. When brokenness overwhelms us, we can lose our vision, senses, and ability to be rational about any situation.

The broken experience that led me to write this book occurred at age 28. It wasn't my first ever broken situation but the most spiritual, physical, emotional, and psychological connection of hurt and remorse I have ever encountered. I just immigrated to the UK to join my husband. The baby I named my heartbeat was my second child, a sweet little genius named Jordan. It was a rough time as I left my family and friends to travel to a strange land I knew little about. I struggled with all the emotions of a loneliness, fear and isolation whilst pregnant. These days I waste no time expressing my love and affection to the child I bore in sorrow. I sometimes ask, Why me? And funnily enough, I am still awaiting an answer; however, God knows the ultimate factors of my life, and he knows the beginning from the end. He also confirmed that his grace suffices to keep me despite all the hardship.

I characterise my personality as a risk taker who can weather the storm in difficult times. Yet, during this period, I hit rock bottom. The pressure was unbearable as I watched my first child struggle to string a sentence together every day. My husband was preoccupied with his new life in a new city. We no longer fellowshipped as a Christian couple; he had left the faith, and that scared me to the point that I went into an instant depression! I felt alone. Nothing made sense. It was like watching a horror film, and I was the main character. I was totally broken, helpless and blinded. I wandered around for years before a glimmer of light shone down my path. It was the magnificent power of God that began to break something in my spirit. I watched my son one morning as he tried to share something that had happened the day before, but he could not get the words out. I became so wrathful in my spirit I called him into my room and began to declare God's power over his life and command that he speak it out in the name of the Lord. The following morning, he spoke with such clarity, a complete sentence. I didn't have to question his speech; it was clear and precise! I burst into excitement, my mourning turned into joy, and I glorified God at that moment. I had just experienced a miracle in my home. Even though I was experiencing this season of brokenness, God was with me, so I persevered. I desperately wanted to share that experience with my husband, but his desire for faith was long gone. I felt rejected and neglected in my faith as my dream of a union with my husband being in church gradually slipped away. His heart was stolen, his vision was blurred, and I was alone. I couldn't control the narrative and was out of my depth. Everything was spiralling out of control; my faith sank to the floor, and my hope dashed into extinction. *'How could this be happening to me?'* I asked myself. At the tender age of fifteen, I gave my heart to the Lord and am a faithful and dedicated Christian woman. I strive daily to reaffirm my vows and refuse to backslide, but now I am facing an unexpected reality.

Life could not possibly get any worse. But it sure did! For years we endured a period of silence, and in a crowded world with our personal peculiarity for comfort, we could not invite people into our surroundings. Because our situation seemed like an isolated case, we were broken, yet it never seemed like the norm for others; it seemed like it was an issue of the weak. Nobody seemed to care that we were silent, and our personal issues kept us bottled up and hidden. We were so deeply crushed by our circumstances that it was hard to speak. My brokenness has stolen years of joy and replaced it with a sense of resentment, abhorrence, and pain.

It was so unbelievable; trying to understand the reality of what was happening; it was mind-blowing. How could this be? The resounding echo of these words pierces my entire being. I cried out in agony, 'God, where are you?' This was no ordinary cry... it shocked my entire being that sent a message to my psyche that alarmed my emotion.

I lost the ability to be rational; I hated my life. How could this be? I was openly and privately rejected by my companion, friend, lover, but most of all, my equal partner. Hatred was the easiest and the only solution to my present struggle that made sense. I hated him with a passion; the betrayal was brutal and, without question, unnatural. It was inhumane. I cannot begin to imagine why and how this could ever be God speaking through me so that his perfect will might be done. I have considered taking the easy option numerous times, packing my bags and leaving the situation, but the Lord kept saying, stay on board; no life will be lost. Enduring hardship is the key ingredient of Christian life because it brings forth fruit ripe for the kingdom (John 16:33),this was an assignment I had to carry by myself. If I fail, how could I say I am his disciple (Luke 14:27). Nonetheless, oftentimes, I felt like God had fallen asleep and I was being punished for some cruel act I can't begin to recall. Then suddenly, the Holy Spirit spoke to me during my time of despair from the life of the Psalmist David, who, in Psalm 55:12–14, expounds on his own encounter of insult in the most unique manner ever. If an enemy insulted me, I could endure it; if a foe rose against me, I could hide. For the first time, it was clear my situation was not isolated; someone had a similar encounter, which gave me hope. It is so unfortunate when you recognise that someone close to you is the adversary the enemy used to hurt you. The devastation of the pain can be unbearable; the impact sends an alarming message to the brain which makes the body react differently to the norm.

In my research, I understand pain is associated with mental health. This was my state of mind, but I didn't know it. According to Mind Charity for Mental Health, mental issues occur when the individual mind fails to cope with issues that affect our emotions. Hence, we find so many people affected without knowing this, but most astonishing was how I survived it. It is nothing shorter than the grace of God that I am alive and still standing in my right mind. This is always my testimony to God to be praised. I am standing in my right mind with the echoing sound of a Hallelujah. Praise God. Despite everything, there is a shout, and I am not ashamed anymore. I was not left alone in my Lo-debar situation. I was pulled by his grace, and today I stand victorious in Christ.

The plan of the enemy was not for me to survive this experience. I recall a threat from the devil; I might have been around 17 years old. As I sat outside under a tree one day, I heard a cold, callous voice scream, 'I will drive you mad!!' As I sat there, I felt the Holy Spirit arise in me. Without thinking, I boldly responded to the threat, affirming, 'your threat will be unfruitful, you are a liar, this will never be my portion, in the name of Jesus,' Glory to God. Hallelujah. I was fearless, remained bold and confident throughout my challenges, and continued to affirm this word that was spoken so many years prior. Hence, I use this opportunity to declare that my God is the all-powerful and self-existent God whose name is Jehovah El Elyon the most high; I just love the sound of his name.

Sometimes we can be the enabler to a broken situation and not know it because of our blind spot, just like the rich ruler, he couldn't see even when it was highlighted. I, too, recognised that I was an enabler of the broken situation that I so desperately tried to escape. The rich ruler could not see that something was missing because his thoughts were preoccupied with his wealth and power that he missed a key ingredient, and so it was with me. I allowed all the negative and painful experiences I faced to rob me of my joy; I refused to accept that there was a better solution than the grief I embraced and was hugging my pain as my safety net, wishing if my circumstances were different, my life would be better. I needed to experience the transferred mindset referred to in Romans 12:2 that encourages us not to become conformed to this world, or its belief, its reality, but to be transformed by the renewing of our mind through Christ Jesus, our Lord. It takes the power of the Holy Spirit to enable such strategic implementation to come back to the enemy's scheme during every broken dream. It took me years to understand what this really meant.

When we think of King David's brokenness and depression, he had no choice but to be strategic to win. The Bible records that the king called out to God, who is his help and strength. He encourages his soul to hope in God (Psalm 43:5). Look also at the life of Jeremiah, the prophet. He, too, was depressed because of constant rejection and loneliness; he was known as the weeping prophet because of his hardship, but look how he was encouraged by God, 'restrain your voice from weeping and your eyes from tears, for your work, will be rewarded, declares the Lord' (Jeremiah 31:16), and verse 3 he says, 'call to me and I will answer you said the Lord.' It can break your spirit when facing a situation that seems like an isolated issue that nobody else has. It is a spiritual force that wars within and creates that imbalance that can only be made whole by prayer and seeking God for his direction.

There is always a period of brokenness in our life. However, after the broken period, there will be a melting before the reshaping and moulding of our designed purpose, whether it be several times or even for a longer time. James 1:2-4 speaks of our testing and how we must seek earnestly to endure to the end; it is only then we will be mature enough to move into the next level that leads to our destiny.

Your experience during your struggle would have taught you everything you need to win, and you won't need anything. The moulding period is never easy; you don't become whole overnight; it's a progressive process that requires determination. I often fall apart, wondering when will I ever surpass this mountain until it hits me like a four-by-four brick. I am not alone. I am my father's child. I know who I am and to whom I belong, so I called out the name my mother gave me, 'Claudia Nicole Brown', and for the first time in years, I understood my purpose. I am my own person, not the product of another.

I ponder these words as I reflect on my testing time when my whole world was falling apart, as if there was no hope. I reaffirm this saying:

'I choose to live by Choice, not by Chance. I chose to make Changes, not Excuses; to be Motivated and not Manipulated; to be Useful but not Used; to Excel, not Compete. I Choose self-esteem, not Self-pity. I Choose to listen to my inner Voice, not the random Opinion of others.' (Anonymous)

The echo of those words allows me to envision a life beyond my struggle.

Though I was only looking through my natural eyes, I am now convinced that God has brought this revelation to my heart in his own perfect way. In an instant, I lifted my hands above my head in total surrender and prayed so humbly.

Prayer

Lord, I confess my fault before thee; I repent as I surrender my will to you. Forgive me, O' Lord. Even though the burden is heavy, Lord, I thank you for the strength to mount this mountain. Lord, I fell off the wagon so many times, it is unbelievable, but thanks be to God, who has helped me to face every day with the mindset that this, too, will pass. Lord, I don't fully understand the processes, but I am counting it all joy as you carry me through. Amen.

I recalled going back, dragging up memories of pain and despair, and these recurrences caused me to lose my faith. As I thought about how easy it was to go back rather than move ahead, the thoughts pulled me apart.

After some time of suffering, I finally came to my senses, just like the prodigal son in Luke 15:11–32.

After sitting in the pigs' wallow, he said 'how many hired servants are there in my father's house with food to spare and here I am eating with the pigs. I will arise and return home.' It was a surreal moment for me when I decided I wanted more. I wanted to move beyond my pain, shame, and disgrace, so I began a new, life-changing habit, reading. Reading was an arduous task, so in developing my analytical skills, I purposefully read a book every week, if possible. I now understand that becoming the person my heart desires would require discipline, so taking on this task was useful to my growth. My circumstances do not determine the quality of my life, but how I process the experience and the learning outcomes mattered.

In my research, I stumbled on the book, *Standing in the Gap* by Johannes Facius. As I read about intercessory prayer and the basic principle of intercession, this scripture unfolded itself. I was astonished by the revelation. The situation will cause you to lose faith (Matthew 18:7). We simply cannot escape it, but how we deal with it is what matters. The circumstances we face produce a certain emotional struggle; however, if we seek to channel our emotions positively, it will change our perspective.

The next verse says, if your hand or your foot causes you to lose faith, cut it off and throw it away. Wow, this is amazing. God was talking straight at me. I wanted that word so badly, but the constant flashbacks, revisiting the painful memories, were too much. I pondered the thought; *I must cut it off and throw it away.* As I think about the strategy for the future, I think of these words. This word must align with my present mindset, but how could I apply it effectively enough to my situation? Sometimes, when the Lord speaks, we need a little time to fully digest the reality of what is being said, and that is exactly how I felt. I understood that the

74

desire to be free from a situation differs from cutting off a grey area of your life.

When one becomes accustomed to rejection, he loses the ability to move beyond that pain. Let's look at the Psalmist David, who shows a different approach towards his brokenness. David delights himself in righteous living and rules justly according to God's divine plan. One writer from the *Daily Bread* devotional guide concluded that, 'these words were noted for people "just like me" who have been wounded, hurt, and rejected but cannot seem to find their way beyond their rejection.' I chose to hold on to these words of comfort because I, too, had been at a place of loss where all I knew was pain but thank God for the Holy Spirit who comes in such might and refreshing power to bind up my broken heart. Today I can testify that his voice makes a difference.

Prayer

Lord, you are a God with a plan (Jeremiah 29:11), and your word declares that it is for good and not evil and will bring forth fruit ripe for the kingdom. Lord, we rejoice in your plan for our lives and continue to boast in the Lord. Amen.

COPING WITH
BROKENNESS IN
THE CHURCH

This chapter reflects on the church's strategic approach to brokenness. We witness God's immense power at work in man's life, bringing forth the transformation of healing and deliverance. The psalmist says a broken and contrite heart, the lord will not despise (Psalm 51:17); his ears are open to their cry. Therefore, this is the church's ministry to minister to the broken and to assist them to lift themselves up in the Lord.

Brokenness is rarely viewed in the positive sense but as a hopeless state, but I can tell you that in your weakness, it is where you are made strong. You might suffer now because of a setback, but you don't realise it might be a set-up for a mighty comeback. Our broken situation is not the end of who we ought to be, but a transition into our God-given destiny. The scripture James 1:2 encourages us to count it all joy when we encounter difficulties because with steadfast faith, knowing that God is in complete control of everything, we have the confidence that all is well, just like the disciples who were out at sea (Mark 6:49-51). When we face trials, we must evaluate the final outcome, knowing whose report we will believe. God can do exceedingly abundantly above all that we can imagine or think (Ephesians 3:20). If our faith is steadfast, then our trials will be met at the foot of the cross, and this is the strategy of the church, to preach hope and declare that all things work for the good of those that love the Lord (Romans 8:28).

The church is a place that promises hope for the broken, hence why it is filled with broken people who have suffered loss, betrayal, grief, and the list goes on, therefore, it is the place where many seek refuge. It is not a strange analysis because it is why Christ came to save those who are lost, broken, rejected, and abused, and he shall find rest in Matthew 11:28-29. Through the ministering of the word, broken lives are made new, and the church is the place to administer such love and security. Unfortunately, we are not all educated or, better yet, skilled to handle some challenges we face because of our lack of knowledge and experience in certain areas as we serve. It really saddened my heart that I wrote this chapter highlighting these factors because the church, which is identified as a place of refuge, is often the last place to find safety for many.

There is no better safe haven than the church, although, many may argue that we lack the basic skills to address the issues that arise. Due to that fact, members suffer in silence and even leave the church with a mental hustle towards the body of Christ. Let this not phase you; the power to heal and bind up the fragmented mind remains in the power of the Holy Spirit.

However, what has happened over the years is that some issues that are brought to the table have never been assessed or structured adequately into our daily routine, but our key tool is continually active, which is to pray. There is a fear that has been argued that as a people, we have adopted the notion that if you are saved, a born-again believer, certain issues are unheard of or forbidden in the church of God. The same attitude was mentioned regarding the man who was born blind (John 9:1-3 NIV). The conclusion was made that he or his parents might have committed a sin for this to happen. But look at

Jesus' response, 'neither this man nor his parents sinned,' but this happened so that the works of God might be displayed in him. We could have thought that the message would have reached home by now. However, unfortunately, we still have this kind of attitude that heavily exists among us, but we continue to pray. Evidence supports this notion that persons are struggling with common issues they are afraid to mention because they fear being judged or cast out from among the brethren. A young convert stood up to testify, and the church laughed at her. She had been a chain-smoker for years. Upon her conversion, she shared this remarkable change of only smoking one pack of cigarettes for the week. That was an impressive achievement for this new convert, but we missed the victory. We could not relate; hence, we judged without compassion.

Why do we operate in unaffectionate manners with real life-changing issues that really affect our lives? Do we forget we live in a real world with issues requiring a practical solution? So, the question, therefore, is why is the church structured in the way it is? Why isn't there not a platform to explore these issues? Most importantly, why are we skirt-tailing around the genuine issues that kill us off as a people? If we are not careful, the next generation will be in trouble. To be precise, we are all spirit-filled but have a physical nature and problems that cannot be ignored. Our people have suffered within the church's walls for far too long. At the same time, we continue to proclaim healing, deliverance, prosperity, growth and a lot of speaking in tongues. Still, we are prisoners of broken dreams and relationships.

Being broken and speaking out can be an isolated road for many, especially when the general congregation does not reflect our personal struggle and pain. I was surprised, after speaking with a brother at church about his own broken experience, as he shared how he felt abandoned as a new believer and a newlywed. He added that the church provided no structural guidance for persons coming into the church who usually practise a different lifestyle to the one they now need to live. We often feel that once we get saved, life is A-okay. We just need to read our bible, pray, and that is it, but what about our social needs? The realities of life and how to live day to day has been widely ignored over the years, and many people have fallen along the way.

The level of brokenness that many of our fellow brothers experience in their marriages, on the job, in ministry, and within society, was a concern for the new believer. It is discouraging to hear that this is happening, but how do we tackle it and address the issue? Jesus answered the question in St. John 9: He showed compassion and ministered to him, and he was healed. Unfortunately, when we are locked down in fear and striving for public approval, we miss the opportunity to be a vessel of honour and quickly relapse to our old ways of doing things rather than addressing the issue. When this happens, people do not see that there is an opportunity for help because there is no door of confidence for advice and guidance.

However, recently, we have been experiencing a shift in the atmosphere where some brave souls have taken up the mantle to tackle them head-on in the spirit of boldness, praise God. We have recently seen where we have become more open and freer to discuss, counsel, fellowship, signpost, and make recommendations while praying into some of the real issues we face today. But how do we move beyond the culture of the norms, and how can we be instrumental to the next generation?

In some of our mega-churches, there are lobby groups in all the ministries to counsel, mentor and advise persons, as we minister to the holistic man. Nothing has changed. Our strategy remains the same as set out by our Lord. However, we have now become wiser, considerate, and more affectionate with each other and learning to be more patient with each other as we pray and seek God for his divine intervention.

For years I felt captive to my brokenness. I left my country to migrate to another where I had no close family, and I struggled to make friends. I was not confident in speaking openly about my situation. I was too afraid to even let people into my life of confusion. However, I give God thanks today, for he has anointed me to share my story and to use it as a catalyst to minister to others. To be an encouragement and role model to those who might suffer but cannot seem to find their way, I am just excited to be considered. I felt like Mary, the mother of Jesus; God (Luke 1:28) highly favoured her, and she expresses her gratitude.

We have often forgotten that our lives are simply not our own. Christ died so we can live and be a blessing to others. What would life be if we had not encountered our own personal challenges? How would we encourage someone else? One person paraphrased the quote by saying 'if I did not have a trial, there would be no testimony' and concluded by saying, 'I give thanks for the experience and lesson learned.' We are encouraged to be thankful for everything and praise the Lord.

Prayer

Heavenly Father, sometimes the storms seem overwhelming, and we often view our situation as an isolated case, but Lord, there is no testing that we face is new to you. Lord, you are Lord of every situation and right now in the midst of the storm we pray you will forgive us of our ignorance and doubt; we confess openly of our error, and we pray as a people that we will trust you, as the body of Christ. Help us not to shift any blame but help us to understand that we are the body of Christ, and our sole duty is to care for each other and show affection to one another. Father, your word declares that we are to confess our faults one to another, treat each other fairly and support each other as we weather the storms in our lives. Help us recognise that our lived experience is the setting stone to mobilise us for greatness in your kingdom. Lord, we depend totally upon you. In Jesus' Holy name, we pray. Amen.

BECOMING A CHASTE VIRGIN

Writing this book is a steppingstone into my God-given destiny, coming into alignment with his plan for my life. The most astonishing experience I have ever encountered is having my dream shattered, and my heart broken by the promises I thought were the real reason for my existence. I never thought that my pain was a part of the process. God had a much-improved plan for my life than I could ever imagine.

During this period, I had more questions than answers, as many of us can attest to when going through a storm. However, I later learned that if I hadn't had that encounter, I wouldn't know the depths of his promise, the fulfilment of his joy, which has shaped my character and has enabled me to share this level of maturity.

Praise be to almighty God that through his favour, he has rescued me from the palm of the enemy's grip and allowed me to be free from guilt, embarrassment, rejection and pain. It's only to him; I give the praise.

Telling the story without revisiting the pain takes complete forgiveness and living a spirit-filled life in Christ Jesus. Without a faith-centred relationship in God, I could not share and encourage others to be faithful, be steadfast, to be unmovable and continue to abound in the promises of God because he never fails (1 Corinthians 15:58).

Without the power of God in my life, it would be impossible to serve from this standpoint, he makes all things new (Revelation 21:5) and because he does, I stand in agreement with the songwriter, and I will follow Christ forward. It's with that level of confidence that I share without intimidation or any ramification because Christ made the difference in my life.

Well, that sounds good and very reassuring for some of us, but not all. Let me encourage you by saying it doesn't matter where you are or what you have been through; if God said it, that settles it. We can draw comfort from these words. It does not matter what others say when you directly encounter God. He tells you that even though you had a curve ball thrown in your life, all will be made new, as though it had never happened; you can't argue that point effectively to win. I am a living testament to that statement. It was a surreal moment when he promised me a Chaste Virgin experience. I had to question the promise, *'What does a Chaste Virgin experience look like, and how can one achieve it?'* It was exceedingly difficult to put into context. I struggled to understand what this really means in the grand scheme of things; one thing was for certain: I had to trust God no matter what, and I had to bury my faith in him. What is so amazing is that God does not wait until the end of the chapter to make things anew. He does it when you accept and surrender your life to his will.

When the Lord spoke to me about the renewed life, the exemplary life of a Chaste Virgin; the depth of the revelation had not yet been revealed. I was desperate for the change. I had not fully understood what a Chaste Virgin experience was about; however, I accepted the words, *'no doubt, these were powerful words to my soul.'*

As time passed, I felt anxious about the word that brought me so much comfort at the outset, but now the more I thought about it, the more the struggle intensified as I sought to accept it. It was as if my mind, body, soul, and spirit refused to believe that my present situation was finally over. I wanted to escape from my prison. All I could think about was laying it down and being at rest. I wanted it over, and I don't believe that is a usual request because every one of us is running or wanting to escape something. However, there is a process in the fullness of time at the appointed time. Let us not become discouraged though the promise tarry; let's wait for it (Habakkuk 2:3).

Years later, the confirmation of those words that brought me such comfort manifested itself in my life; as clarity came through the scripture from Joel 2:25 AMP) 'The Lord says, "I will give you back what you lost to the stripping locusts, the cutting locusts, the swarming locusts and the hopping locusts,"' For a moment, I experienced surreal encounters with the past and the promise. All of my present emotions erupted, as I reflected and analysed the situation. There were moments when I sat in silence as I was unsure how I'd go forward. As an intercessor, I did what I do best; I prayed into this lived experience, and the story of Job came to mind. Job answered God's questions by saying, 'I had heard about you before, but now I've seen you with my own eyes. So, I take back everything I said, and I'll sit in dust and ashes to show I'm sorry' (Job 42:5-6). This experience could have paralysed me and blown my mind. Still, I entered into a full-blown God moment. I had to repent because I then understood that this struggle, this brokenness, was far beyond flesh and blood. It was God himself that could ever bring the relief my heart so desperately needed. I saw my shattered life and God's hand at work for the first time in years. All the complaining, crying, and asking God why I was going through all this trouble made sense.

My heart rested as Job did when God restored him beyond his previous status (Job 42:10).

As the revelation unfolded, I bowed in true repentance before God. His ways are higher than mine, his thoughts are greater than mine, and his plan for me is so much better than I thought it could have been, and there I surrendered. There was no shouting or motivational speech, music playing in the background to build up this moment of truth; it was the Holy Spirit at work within.

Although, I felt refreshed and renewed I knew that the battle had just begun at another level. First, I had to dig deep into God's arms and hide under his coverage to maintain my strength. Then, when I thought it was time to sit back and relax, reality hit home. The battle has now escalated to another level, and the force of darkness has become more brutal and intense than I could ever imagine.

It was no surprise that I felt this way. It's a common emotional battle we all feel as we navigate our storms. Many of us often face this challenge and fall along the way because we expect a happy-go-lucky lifestyle, which is never the reality. The complaining mentality kicks in again, and I struggled to face the reality of my situation, but I love how the Holy Spirit speaks. He is so profound and clear, can never be misunderstood. He says when our deliverance comes; it doesn't mean our fight is over. It is only the beginning. I must be prepared to fight to maintain victory.

The desire to have God's will manifested in my life was my only hope of escape. Therefore, I hold on to the promise of the Chaste Virgin experience; I must remain pure and faithful to the Lord and keep hold of his promises that echo in 2 Corinthians 5:17 'all things will be made new.' Because I knew that my life is hidden with Christ in God (Colossians 3:3), I knew then that my marriage belongs to God, he honours our union, his promise is clear and though the enemy tried his tricks to implant doubt, God's promise is faithful, and I needed to hold it. The enemy continues to influence my thoughts with negative comments, and I struggled, based on my human ability, to deal with past hurts and painful memories. It was a fight to the finish to be free.

As I ponder these words, I reflect on the scripture that speaks of the Sower and the seeds. Some fall on good ground, others fall on stony ground, and others fall among thorns in the story. The seed in the story depicts our deliverance; the enemy continues to seek ways to destroy the gift and abort the plan of God for our lives, but then we have to be strategic and persevere in our faith and be courageous.

The fights we face daily are not just physical but spiritual as the enemy seeks every opportunity to break our spirit and to cause chaos in our lives; hence, we need to continue to tap into the presence of the Lord for strength to endure to the end. It was then the reality hit home that my fight was not physical as I thought, but spiritual, and now I needed to tap into the word of God. I was forced to declare his promises over my life, his plan for me to succeed and be in good health. I had been predestined before I got here, and no plan of the enemy can prevail against it (Romans 8:35-39). *If you are experiencing any such encounter today, I bind it up in the name of Jesus. 'Be strong and courageous. Do not be terrified; do not be discouraged, for the LORD your God will be with you wherever you go' (Joshua 1:9).*

This experience of a Chaste Virgin revelation occurred while I was on my way to an early morning prayer meeting, as I reflected on my husband's efforts to reconcile our marriage after years of abuse, rejection, and neglect. I thought, *am I strong enough to accept his offer to reconcile? Can I truly forgive? Is there a future after this, and what would it look like?* These are just a few of the questions that challenged my thoughts. Our marriage had encountered a silent moment of brokenness of trust that had shaken the foundation upon which we stood. After years of praying and seeking God for divine intervention, my husband had now come to a place where he recognised the consequence of his actions and now wanted to make amends. The scripture that came to thought was Matthew 18:21–22, where Jesus said we ought to forgive, but the question echoing in my mind was, *"How can I?" Was I dreaming?* Even though I had prayed earnestly for this moment, then the word came. Forgiveness was not necessarily for my husband, but for my healing. It was an *odd moment that blew my mind.* Harbouring resentment was not healthy, and it was a fuel to my pain. I wanted to move beyond the pain, but I struggled a bit with the concept of letting go, pardoning the wrong, and giving him a second chance. I felt like he was getting away with murder. We often feel that way as humans.

We all want to exercise revenge on the one who hurt us, especially if it is a recurrent practice, but the word of God is teaching us to forgive as much as we expect our Heavenly Father to forgive us.

It may be difficult for most of us as we learn the meaning of forgiveness, which is understandable, in God's plan, things work differently. During this process, we must dig deep down in prayer and supplication as we make our request known. Philippians 4:6 states that God's plans are never up to us; what I wanted and what God had in store are completely different.

It fascinates me every time I reflect on the caring rebuke of the Holy Spirit. Somehow, I just love the rebuke of the Holy Spirit. There is no other option but to surrender to his will because he is so moderate in his approach. He is so mild and warm in his action; he will not argue; he simply reinforces the ultimate plan. His agenda is to help and guide us into our true destiny and purpose when God rebukes us. He is direct, and his tone is friendly and kind and very much encouraging.

When we look at the word rebuke, the English Dictionary implies to be reprimanded or scolded, with a verbal approach to be stern. That interpretation gives a reflection of being harsh or angry at someone. However, this is not the nature of the Holy Spirit. On the contrary, he is kind, gentle and comforting. He is our teacher, helper, and counsellor; his aim is to lead and guide us to live as God's children (Hebrews 12: 5-6); his rebuke is necessary for our growth and development. Therefore, if we want to reap the benefit of his glorious intervention, it is in our best interest to comply.

The revelation was a dreamlike encounter. In his own gentle way, he spoke to me and said, 'my husband will be whole again.' The message was obvious: the past will be rewritten as though it never happened. I never thought this was possible. This was an unknowledgeable thought; I have never heard of it before or have any inclination that it was a biblical term used by the apostle Paul in 2 Corinthians 11:1-2. In fact, the revelation was so profound that the Lord confirmed it in an instant, minutes after. It was astonishing.

On the journey to wholeness a significant encounter with the past is required, it is a steppingstone to a glorious, brighter, better, and triumphant tomorrow.

Let's look at where the apostle explains the transformation of the past into the present and the future tense to believers at Corinth. First, Paul reminded the believers of their past behavioural conduct, how God used him to minister to them, and how the transformation took place. He was worried about their presence, the struggle of an interfering spirit that might try to influence their minds and cause them to return or to be held captive by some strange doctrine. This is the enemy's whole duty, to enslave us either through the bondage of broken and crushed relationships or past failure or personal inability. He will stop at nothing to get us to remain in that status of bondage. So, in his best effort, Paul recalled who they were without God. And through the power of the Holy Spirit, Christ, by repentance, they were converted back to God as chaste and virginal (2 Corinthians 11:2).

The brethren at Corinth were not the only people to experience the Chaste Virgin experience. Before she experienced the conversion of a chaste virgin, the woman at Simon's house, who washed the feet of Jesus with her tears and wiped them with her hair, had a very colourful lifestyle. The scripture recorded that she was a prostitute, a sinner, and an outcast. At Simon's house, she met Jesus. Her life changed dramatically since that very hour (Luke 7: 47). Years of brokenness, emptiness, suppression, and a byword to those who knew her all changed in one encounter at Jesus' feet. Finally, she was made entirely whole (Luke 7:50), 'Your faith has saved you. Go in peace.' What an amazing transformation unfolding before our eyes, with only one visit to the specialist who knows all about our cares and understands our pains. The woman's fractured life had been made whole again. She was no longer identified as the woman of the past but was one who dedicated her life to the ministry of Christ after her conversion (Matthew 27:55-56).

Some theological scholars have depicted the story of Mary Magdalene as a sinful woman. However, in Luke 7:36-50 it doesn't matter who she is or isn't, the most important thing is her life has changed. A woman classified as an outcast, demon-possessed, but thanks be to almighty God, she had the revelation and the encounter of a chaste virgin.

The scripture speaks so eloquently about who is a virgin. According to the bible dictionary, a virgin is classified as an unmarried woman, who is of marrying age and not sexually involved with the opposite sex. Studies reveal that in some cultures, if an unmarried female is identified as not being a virgin, the consequence could be heavy on the family. However, from a Christian perspective, the same view is measured slightly differently, especially when we evaluate the concept of a chaste virgin. Again, though our sins may be scarlet, they shall be made as white as snow; if we accept the Lord Jesus Christ as our personal saviour, everything that we know, or others know about us can be made new in Christ. According to the scriptures, a virgin is viewed as pure, untouched and without spots or wrinkles. That is precisely what a direct encounter with Christ Jesus brings to a broken and crushed life.

In his letter of encouragement, Paul asked the brethren to put up with a bit of foolishness as he explained his reasons for being so overprotective over their souls. However, he was aware of his duties as a brother in the body of Christ and the labour of love he undertook to bring them to Christ as a spotless virgin for him (2 Corinthians 11:2).

When the Lord spoke to me about the renewed life of a chaste virgin, the depth of the revelation had not yet been revealed to me in its totality. I accepted the word without hesitation; however, the more I reflected, the more the enemy tried to discourage me, but I refused to accept defeat. This was my moment, my entry point to a complete breakthrough.

It took another ten years to truly experience this promise of the Chaste Virgin. Finally, on our 25th wedding anniversary, we renewed our vows, the same vows we had pledged a quarter century earlier. The power of God was felt in our presence, and amongst our guests, it was utterly amazing. Everyone present witnessed the power of God as he mended our broken marriage and made all things new.

Although the battle continued beyond my expectation, God had a victory shout awaiting us. Though we have suffered with this condition for many years, our jubilee, to break free had come; the enemy wouldn't let it happen without a fight. The enemy did not want us to escape the prison we had grown accustomed to; he wouldn't let us go without a fight.

Pharaoh challenged Moses in his effort to keep the children of Israel in captivity, yet, through faith in the true and living God, Pharaoh and his army met their demise. The woman with the issue of blood was bound by her infirmity, but with God's divine grace, she found the strength to push through every obstacle to emerge from that prison. These testimonies remind us that God's hands are always open to deliver us from death, no matter how serious the problem or how far we have fallen in oppression.

Prayer

Heavenly Father, thank you for the power of forgiveness, the strength to trust your leadership and the courage to accept that all is well because your grace is indeed sufficient.

We thank you for our confidence in you, the promise of new hope and a fresh anointing. Lord, we stand before you humbly at your throne as we show gratitude for the renewed life, we have in you. Lord, this renewed life has given us hope and hope that has not made us ashamed (Romans 5:5). We thank you and give you praise in Jesus' name. Amen.

NEWNESS
HAS ARRIVED

A s I struggled to free myself from the confines of my brokenness, I stood triumphant as a follower of Christ and his promises in my life. I resisted the forces of darkness and the demonic tactics of contempt. I am standing fast with my loins girded with the gospel of truth after learning of his goodness and grace. Being confident of this, that he who began a good work in you will carry it on to completion, (Philippians 1:6). I comprehend the importance of reaffirming God's divine plan for my life. To escape, I accepted it rather than just hearing it; mountains that stood still and firm for years cracked. I knew then that for me to survive, an active motion of faith in action should be displayed both in the spirit and in the natural. There had to be a shift in the atmosphere.

Many things transpired once I decreed and declared God's promises. I have likened this experience to a woman in labour. Imagine, after hours in pain, the hour to deliver draws nearer. Then the reality hits home that the true fight for life has just begun, 'the pushing experience.' There is no joy in pushing because it drains your energy. Studies show that a woman can give birth within three hours of active pushing. Imagine the energy and the pain, but the process brings the greatest joy. A new life has been born. It is a season of new beginnings. Greater opportunities lay ahead, but there has to be a pushing. No one can experience a new life without pushing or pulling. During that time, the muscles are being exercised to give mobility and strength to joints. Everything that breathes has to be pushed or pulled. We see Jesus pull the cross to the hill to breathe newness into man.

In order to win, we have to be determined to be a pusher, having a 'won't stay down attitude,' and a willingness to keep going as a true survivor. My brokenness had brought me to a place of hopelessness; but then I realised that in order to survive, I had to get up and push. I wanted to live. I wanted to look back at this experience and say, God, had it not been for your grace, I would not have made it. It was during my time of pushing that restoration had given birth to hope, to peace, and to joy in the Holy Ghost.

The newness of life was arising, but I had to contend with that end result. I had to dig deep now into prayer otherwise, it could not be possible without active prayer, fasting and trusting God for direction. Every day, I had to affirm my faith that this experience could not and would not be wasted. It is an uphill struggle, but you must remain focussed and steadfast in everything. You will experience doubt and fear of the unknown, prior struggles will resurface, and you will feel the pain you have gone through as though it were a brand-new experience. But we have to trust in the Lord.

To win, you must understand the concept of new birth; there has to be an active force of pushing. According to the Free Medical Dictionary (online), giving birth involves a heavy pushing against the odds, a coming into being the act or process of being born. The process describes the separation of the infant from its maternal body by cutting the umbilical cord and it is the same procedure followed in the spirit world. There must be a separation (1 Peter 1: 23) for you have been born again, not of perishable seed, but of imperishable, through the living and enduring word of God. In the process of birth, something new has to take place, and the progress has an appointed time in which it ought to happen (Job 14:5). We can't waste time thinking it should be any sooner. If it is, it will be prematurely born outside its appointed time and encounter great difficulties.

I was naïve about the concept of my deliverance for a while, until I came face to face with the true revelation of the pushing process. Another missed concept was within the word, as I thought my deliverance meant the end of my fight. I thought the fight was over and all was well, as in the fairy tale stories, my happy-ever-after mentality.

Later I understood it was the beginning of a new fight to keep that which had been promised. As I thought about this, the story of David came to mind; he was a young boy when he was anointed to be king. However, it didn't manifest until he was 30 years old (2 Samuel 5:4). Samuel anointed David to be king. Still, years went by before the promise was revealed. This fight to maintain the promise also involved a time of waiting and being faithful despite everything. This process can be easily missed if we are not careful because of our anxiety and lack of faith. The Bible urges us to maintain our faith, even when everything appears hopeless. Knowing that God directs the righteous actions (1 Timothy 1:19), Habakkuk 2:3 says to 'wait for the vision, while it tarries.' No matter how dismal our situation appears, God has a plan in everything for his glory that I did not fully understand for a while. But I really adored the way the Holy Spirit functions. In my moment of confusion, he spoke very profoundly. He said, 'this is your moment of release, and I must fight for it,' wow!

Those words changed my perspective straight away. The word was quickly confirmed by the scripture, Jude urged the brethren to battle for their faith in verse three, saying, 'Fight for what you believe, trust God with all your heart, and don't allow nothing or anything to change your thinking in the Lord.' I now understand what Jude meant by this. As people of God, we often miss the opportunity to occupy or cease it because our outlook differs, and we do not have the basic understanding of how God moves. Too often, we try to rationalise what God intends, and that is where we get it all wrong. I now understand that when deliverance comes, I am responsible for fighting to keep it because the enemy continues to formulate a strategy to plunder the inheritance of God's children.

Entering newness means celebrating, giving thanks, and praising God for what he has done. On our 25th wedding anniversary, the thought of celebrating the journey seemed clear through our physical eyes. Still, as the day drew near, we experienced the spiritual element at work. Something new began to birth in our lives.

We had missed years, months and weeks of not sharing an intimate space in the presence of the Lord. As we started to take baby steps, the unnatural things of the past suddenly became natural again; our desire to pray together was restored, our conversation became so much more fruitful, and our relationship grew daily as we learned these basic rules afresh.

My husband had struggled for years to pray aloud or even to join hands together to invoke the presence of the Lord in our home. The enemy tried to mute him and keep him bound, but God had given birth to a new revelation, and we continue to strive to keep that newness alive. Praise God!

We need not ask why it took all these years before we could enjoy this time together, one thing for sure 'count it all joy, my brothers, when you meet trials of various kinds, for you know that the testing of your faith produces steadfastness.

And let steadfastness have its full effect, that you may be perfect and complete, lacking in nothing' (James 1:2–4).

Jeremiah 29:11

For I know the thoughts that I think toward you, saith the Lord, thoughts of peace, and not of evil, to give you an expected end.

Prayer

Lord, thank you, for your grace and strength. Lord there were times I felt as though I would not make it to this hour, but you kept me. You continue to reassure me that your grace is indeed enough for me. Thank you, Lord, for making all things new, for restoring the brokenness that stole my joy today. I embrace your wholeness in our union, and we will follow you forward. Heavenly Father, we trust the new adventure, the new challenges, the new assignment, and your faithfulness that will enable us on this journey. Lord, we give you thanks. Amen.

TESTIMONY
OF GROWTH

'I call you from the ends of the earth when my heart is weak. Lead me to the rock that is high above me' (Psalm 61:2). 'The Lord Himself goes before you; he will be with you. He will never leave you nor forsake you. Do not be afraid or discouraged' (Deuteronomy 31:8).

We often forget these quotes when the rubber really hits the road. We often forget who is truly in control of our entire existence and that he knows the beginning from the end and that he is working things out for our good.

I won't pretend, I too suffered with this concept. I pray that someone somewhere out there has the answer. When I feel like this, I often feel the urge to find someone apart from God to offload my troubles, forgetting that there is an open invitation to look to God, who is my source of life.

We all want someone to offer us that 'get-out-of-prison ticket' because we feel the Lord is taking too long to come to our rescue. I was so wrong! The Lord's ways are not ours, neither is his timing. He is never late. He will perform his plan of action at the appointed time. I reflect on some promises that God made to his people. It amazes me how long the fulfilment took before it became a reality into the lives of those to whom it was promised. In Hebrews 11, we see the champions of faith walk believing God for the promise that was foretold and die without seeing it, yet they believed and held fast to his word. They are our example to trust the Lord during our time of testing that he knows what his best and will make all things new, only if we believe!

For years I struggled to do what the Lord has put in me because of fear. I also tend to ignore the pounding urge to write, a suppressed gift that went undeveloped and ignored for years. God has not forgotten the talent that he sowed in you or me; so that we can use it to glorify his kingdom. Though the gift takes time to manifest itself, I encourage you to please wait for the appointed moment. The challenges we face are not part of a sprint whereby we are destined to win but a marathon where we learn and develop as we endure to the end.

Discouragement seemed to breathe at every counter and junction of my life and helped to bury my talent beneath all my broken dreams and struggles. I've attempted the 'chasing game,' as I call it, in which I try to blend in with social circles, networks, occupations, relationships, and conversations, but never found fulfilment, joy, or acceptance. I kept going around in circles, trying to find my light, my place of acceptance, only to discover that it was there all the time, and I didn't recognise it. My years were spent trying to live up to other people's standards and expectations, not knowing that each person is unique and that no two people are the same. We might have similar traits, but nothing remains identically. God was direct and specific when I was made in secret, intricately woven in the depths of the earth (Psalm 139:15), Wow! He knew me, he saw me, and he discerned my thoughts. He is acquainted with all my ways even before I speak, God knows, that really speaks volumes to my life.

My identity has been restored, there was no doubt even though I was incredibly young, naïve and inexperienced, when I first encountered this level of brokenness that held me captive for years. God had noted everything about me in his book, and his plan for my deliverance could not be aborted.

I didn't know who I was, my purpose, or my vision. Everything was blurry. Nothing was coordinated. *Who am I?* The voice within continued to cry out. It was confusing, I thought I was a wife, and that was my sole duty; but then I felt empty, unfulfilled, angry, disappointed, crushed, rejected and broken. Life was not fair. The thought of shame and abandonment unsettled me, yet I remained faithful. I endured all the negative stigmas. My point of reference unrecognisable and I needed change. Even if it killed me, I was determined to escape, even if it cost me my life. I knew a treasure was locked inside me, and I was prepared to discover it. Nothing was going to stop it!

In 2018, I took a cruise with my sons and a few friends to the Caribbean. I knew something was happening to me on the inside. I felt a shift; a beam of light penetrated my darkness. Change was aroused within me. I just didn't understand the process; I was in transition, my time had come, and I knew God had a plan.

As I boarded the aircraft in Miami, heading home after an eventful holiday, I sat relaxing and thinking about the journey ahead. As I scrolled through the entertainment channels trying to occupy my time, the Holy Spirit spoke to me. A routine trip turned into something I least expected. I felt the urge to offload on my friend, but that wasn't the option God had in mind. The yearning and desire to pen my emotions compelled me, an enlightening moment that I can't really put into words, and so, the script flowed.

God has a divine plan for our life; we often utter these words loosely, but have we stopped to consider the pros and cons of what we say? The strategic element is to seek a way and means to activate God's plan. He won't come down and do the work for us. There must be a willingness to move from our disposition to move into God's divine plan.

In that moment, I recognised what the Lord wanted me to do: take charge, be responsible for my destiny and be accountable for the direction of my life. My eyes were then opened, and I understood the mystery behind my calling. The CEO of my life is me. I control how I allow the external factors of life to affect me. I don't live by the standard of another but by his precept, he who is the source of my life.

As I lifted my head, I smiled in my heart, God created me to be who I am in his will. I decided to push through my struggle and share my story. I refused to live any longer as a product of brokenness. I am free, I am delivered, and I have found my place.

Thank you, Jesus.

Prayer

Lord, Today we embrace wholeness, we thank you that during our weakness; we are made strong. Thank you, Lord, that we can share our stories of victory in confidence with others and tell of your goodness with purpose. Lord, our experience has taught us many lessons, but most of all, it taught us to trust you despite all the odds, and we are so grateful for that assurance. Lord, we glorify you. We pay homage to your unfailing love. Thank you, Lord, for everything and for giving us the courage to share. Continue to pour out your anointing as we wait patiently in Jesus' name. Amen!

CONCLUSION

E ven though I had a wonderful revelation from God (2 Corinthians 12:7), the fight was real. The struggle became intense. There and then I had to know who I was and to whom I belonged. When I felt so alone, I cried out to God. I was still confused, but I kept my hope alive by reading his word. I felt the anguish of Paul's frustration as he cried out to God regarding the thorn in the flesh. Three different times, I begged the Lord to take it away. Each time he said my gracious favour is all you need. My power works best in your weakness (2 Corinthians 12:8–9). This word had become my declaration and my constant reminder of my purpose and faith in God.

When I think back, I remember the promise made to Caleb. After 45 years, he stood confidently and boldly in front of Joshua and the Israelites to claim his inheritance (Joshua 14:6-15). The fight to claim the promise was still alive then, as it was when he first had the promise made to him by Moses (Joshua 14:10-11). The Lord has given me this promise that everything will be made anew. As stated in my earlier chapter, I received the word of promise with great expectation. I was desperate, and I needed this change, but instead of things getting better, I had to go through a lonely process of hardship and discouragement.

The rejection didn't stop, and I still had trouble with my self-esteem. My confidence was at its lowest, and it stayed that way for a few more years. However, God remained faithful. I began to open up to persons with whom I had now gained confidence; I proclaimed positive affirmation over my life, and I spent quality time in the presence of the Lord. My relationship with the Lord needed to be strengthened. I was making minor improvements, but I recognised that there was a need for a more profound encounter with God. Spending time in prayer was vital to the promise. During this time, I could encapsulate all the emotional pain I had suppressed over the years. I brought them to the Lord in prayer. I needed a deeper intimate moment with God where I was not afraid to give all my brokenness, shame, rejection, and pain. As a result, I was made whole, renewed, and refreshed; I could only achieve this through a time of fasting and prayer.

This process has no microwave solution. We must be mindful that your present situation didn't happen overnight; therefore, breaking free will take some time, especially if you accept your failure as normal. I had to rely on God's word and his promise for my life and dismiss every interfering thought of the enemy. The scripture that helped me was 2 Timothy 2:15. I had to study the word of God and began to speak in confidence to enable me to stand during the tough times.

The moral of my story is to encourage others that though we are saved and believing Christians, we suffer hardship, broken vows, rejection, and pain, but God is faithful. Matthew 28:20b 'I will be with you always, even until the end of the world,' and at my very lowest point this scripture became my safety net. Even though Christ was talking about making disciples, those words kept me when I felt all alone. Each time I echo those words, it is as if God was saying 'you can do this, this situation won't kill you, you are more than a conqueror, and most importantly my grace is indeed sufficient to keep you' (2 Corinthians 12:9). My readers, I encourage you, to hold fast to your faith in God; know who you are in him. Even if your vision becomes blurry, trust him, his plan is to give us an expected end (Jeremiah 29:11).

Be encouraged!

www.marciampublishing.com

Printed in Great Britain
by Amazon

37809998R00079